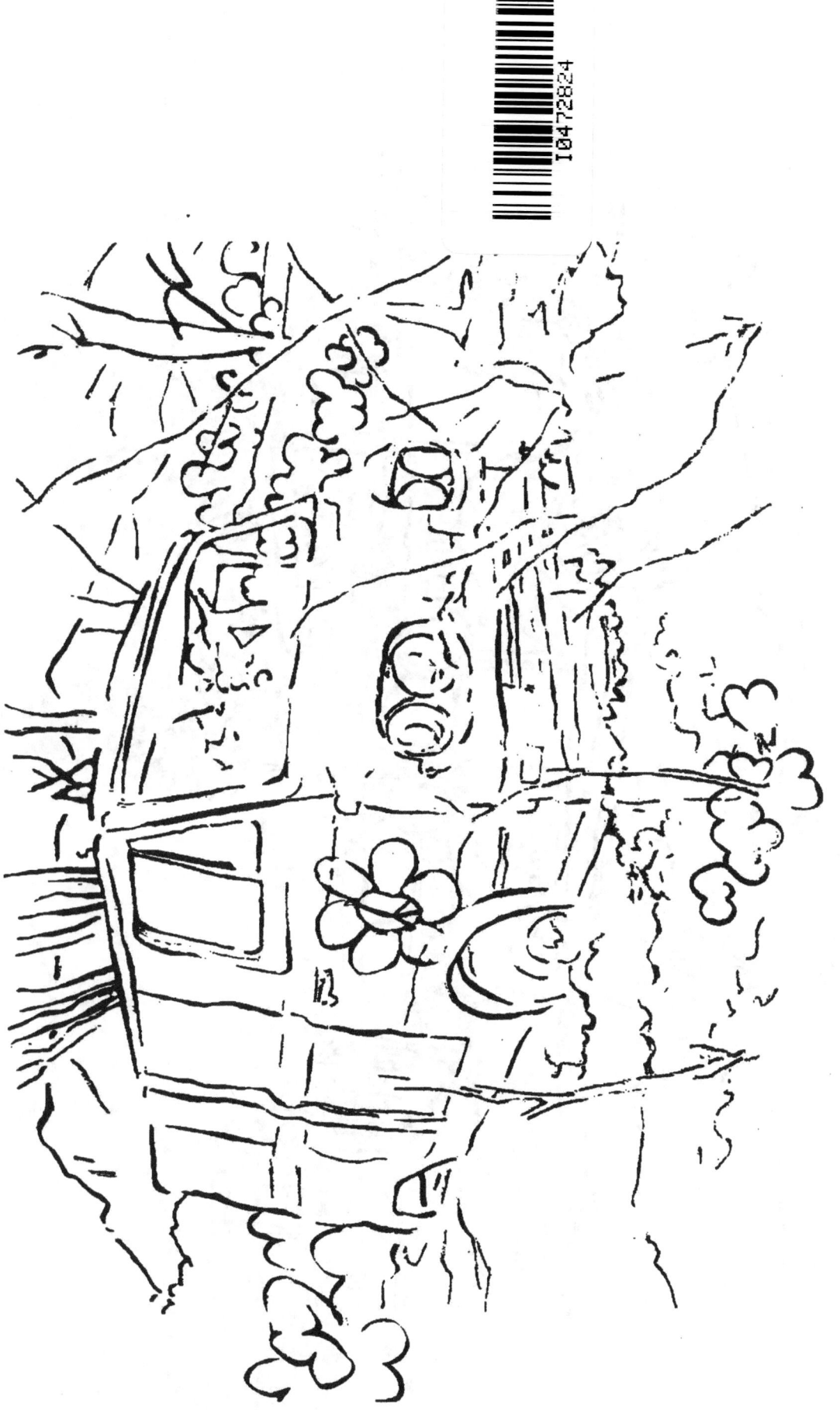

These rusted relics seem to live in harmony with nature.

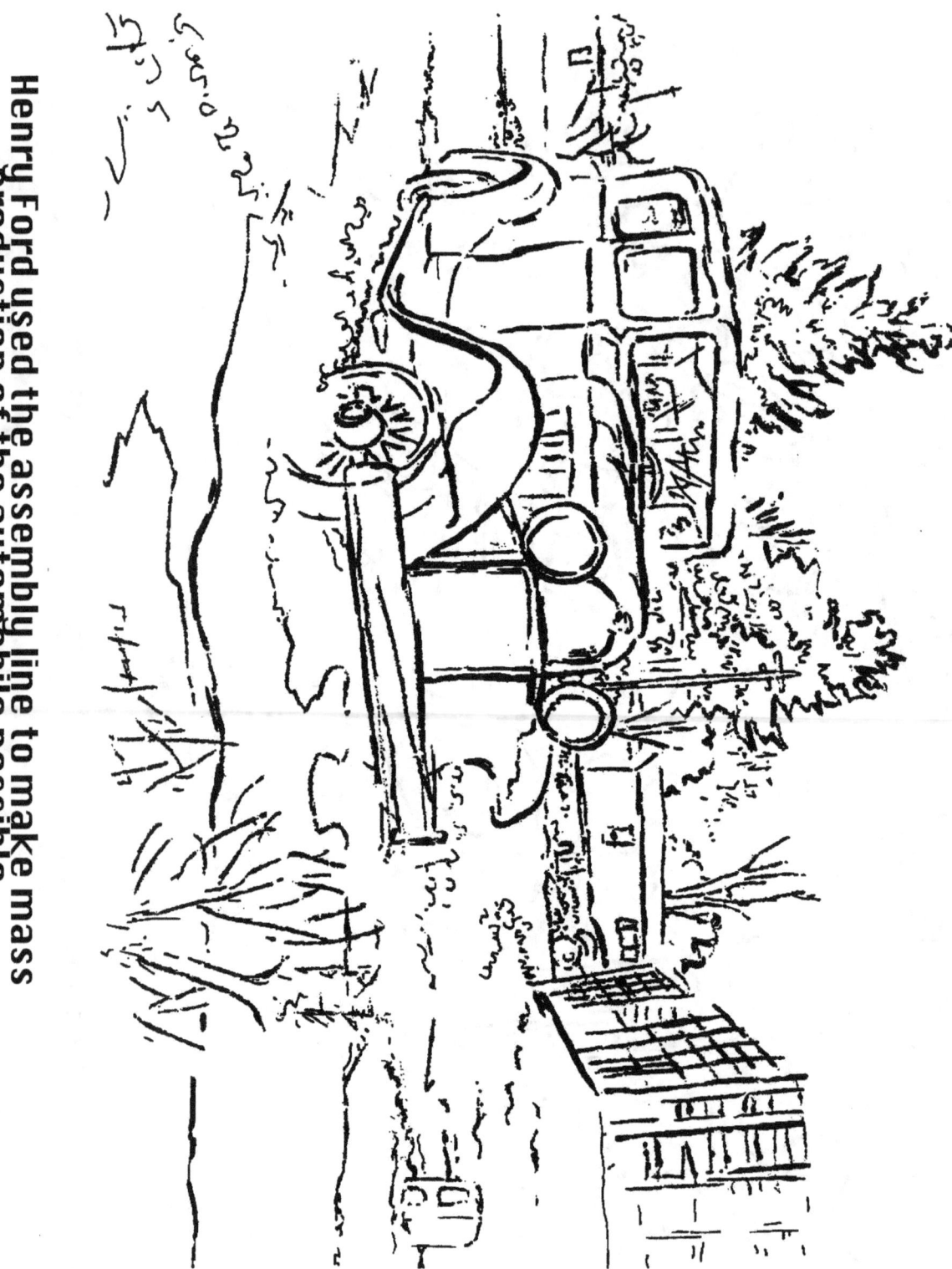

Henry Ford used the assembly line to make mass production of the automobile possible.

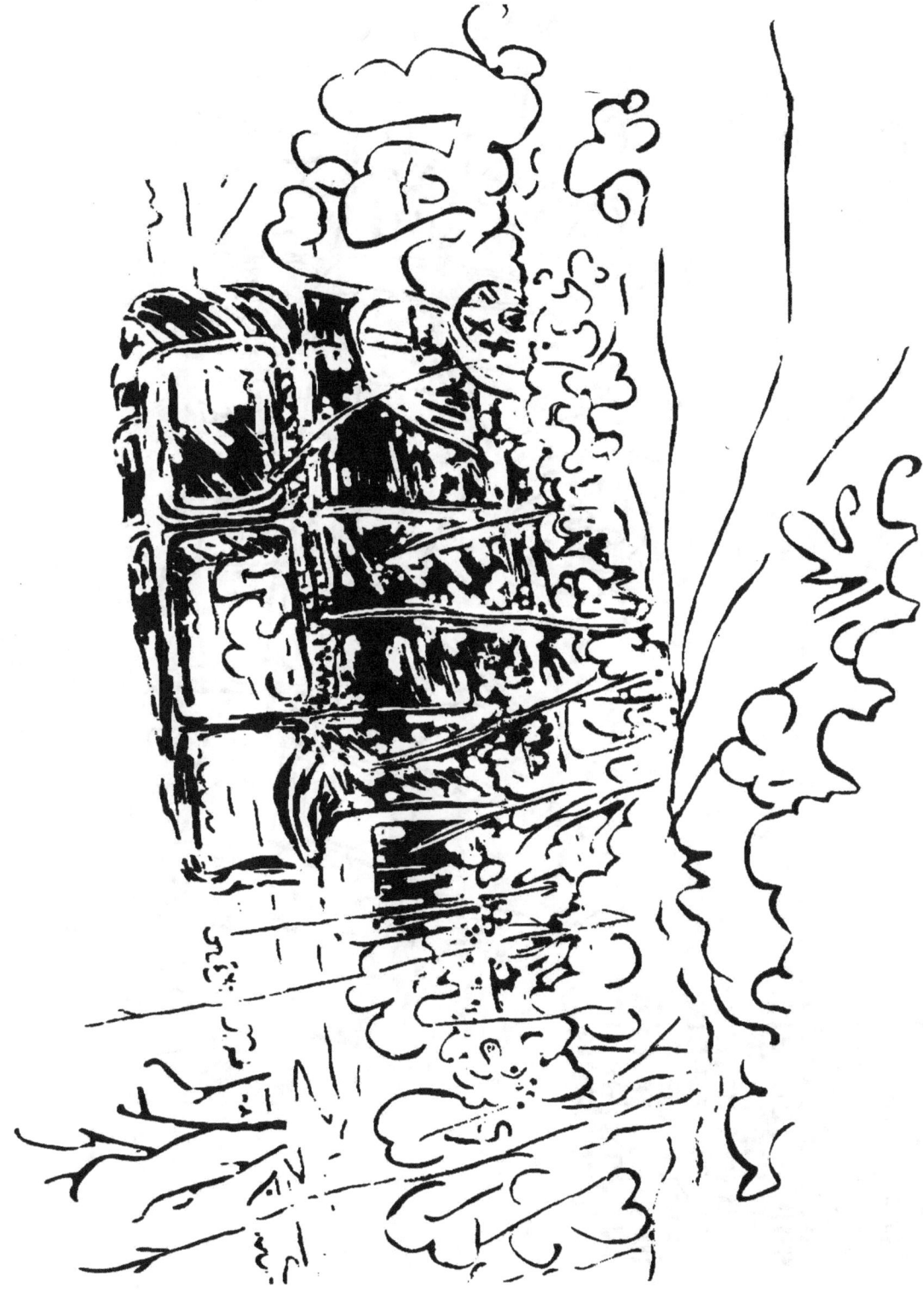

Ford manufactured 15 million Model T's, most of them black. The cars were affordable, so soon, many families could own one.

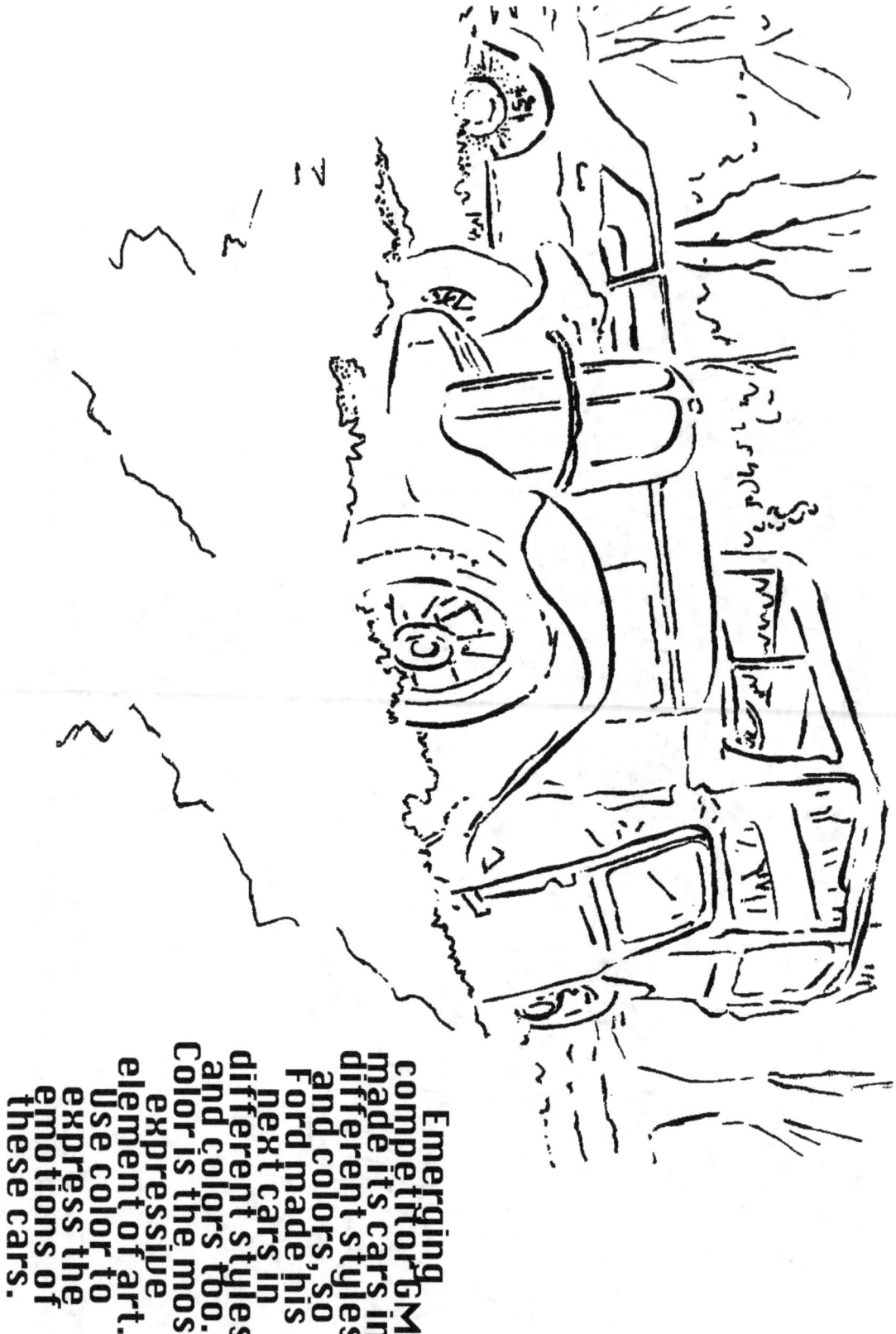

Emerging competitor GM made its cars in different styles and colors, so Ford made his next cars in different styles and colors too. Color is the most expressive element of art. Use color to express the emotions of these cars.

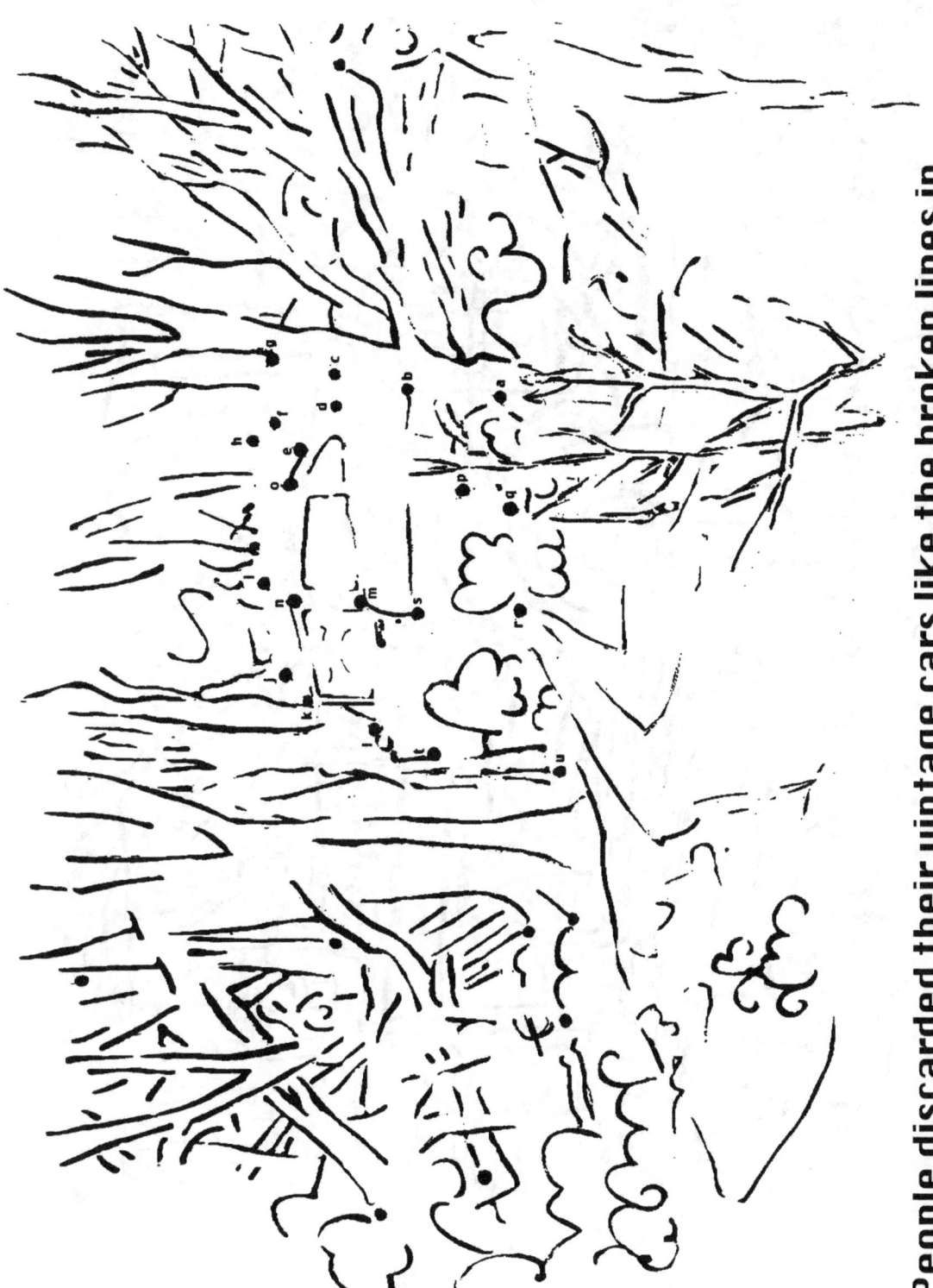

People discarded their vintage cars like the broken lines in this picture. You know what to do to restore this wreck!

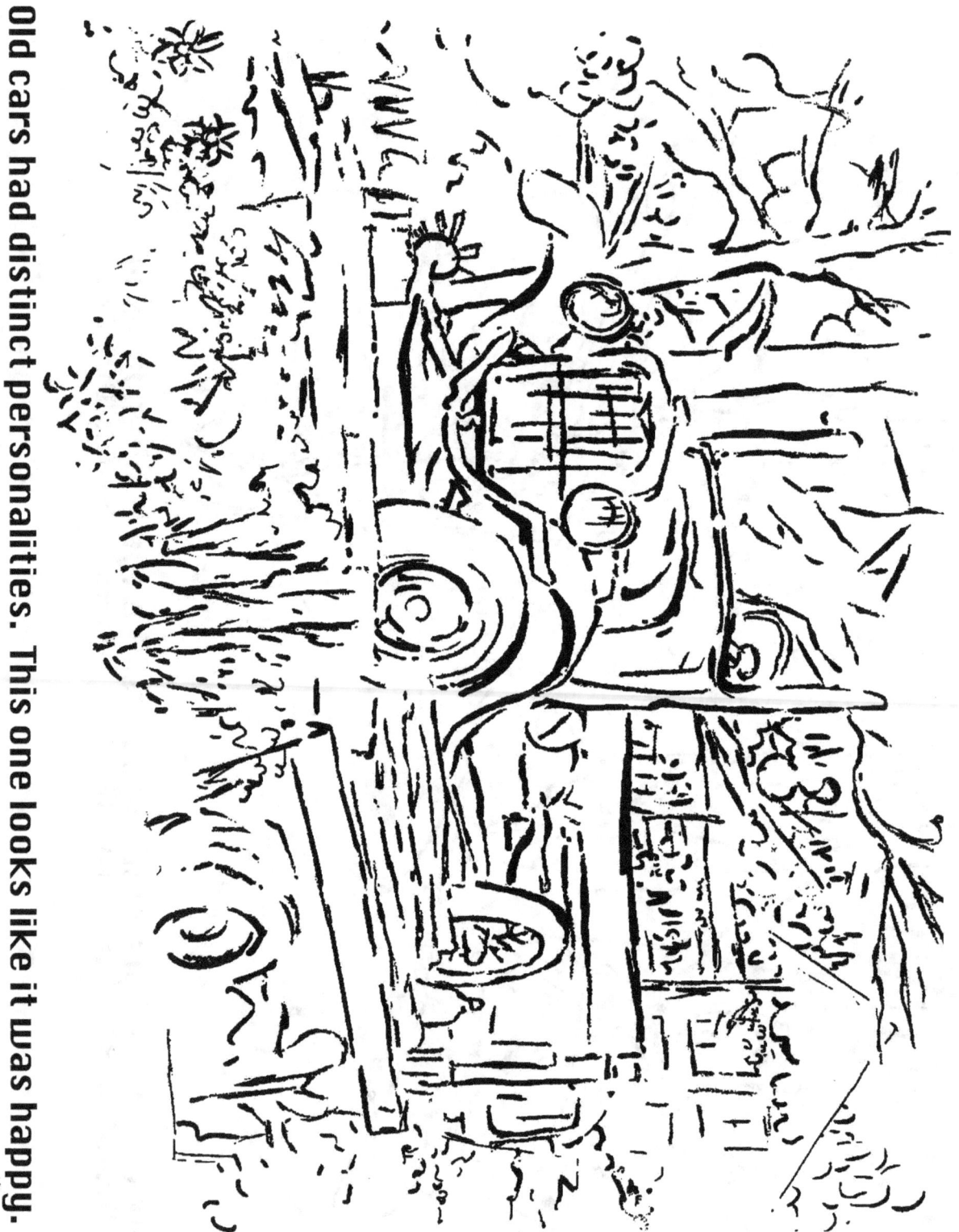

Old cars had distinct personalities. This one looks like it was happy.

This old car may look like junk.

© 2010

But to a collector, it's a valuable investment.

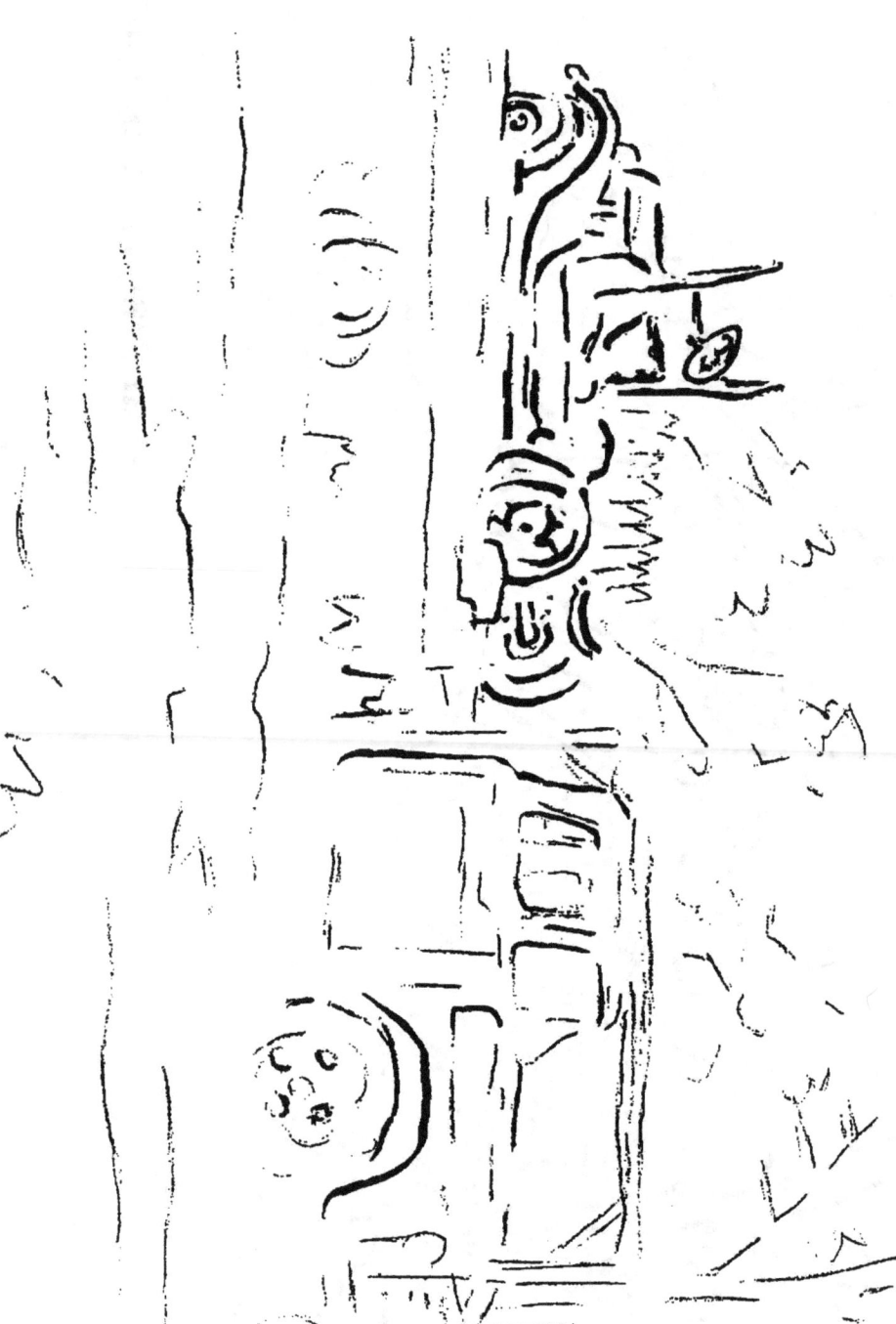

© MM

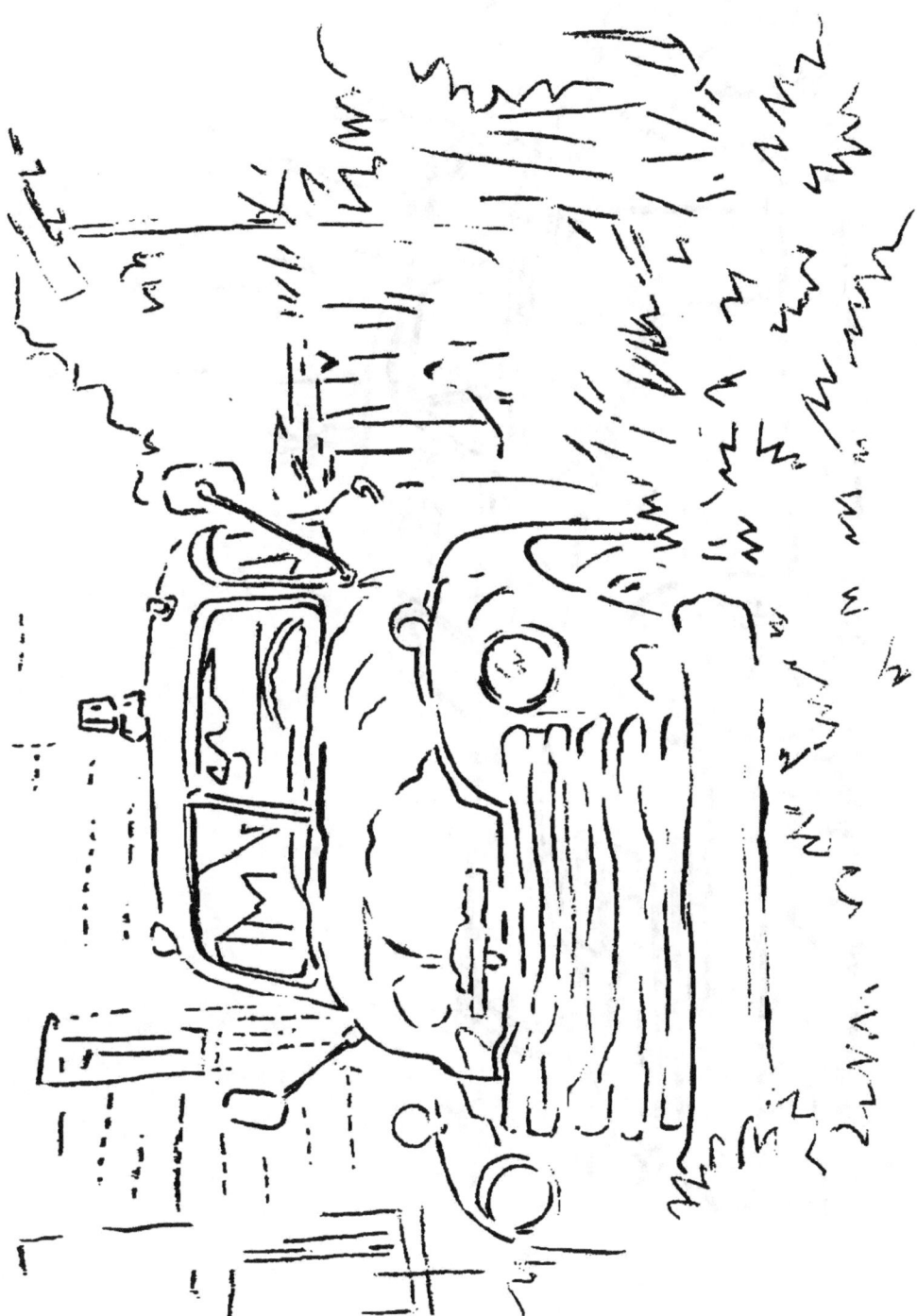

This fire engine pays tribute to all the generous Americans who sacrifice their lives for others.

Some people think 1950s cars looked like bubbles.

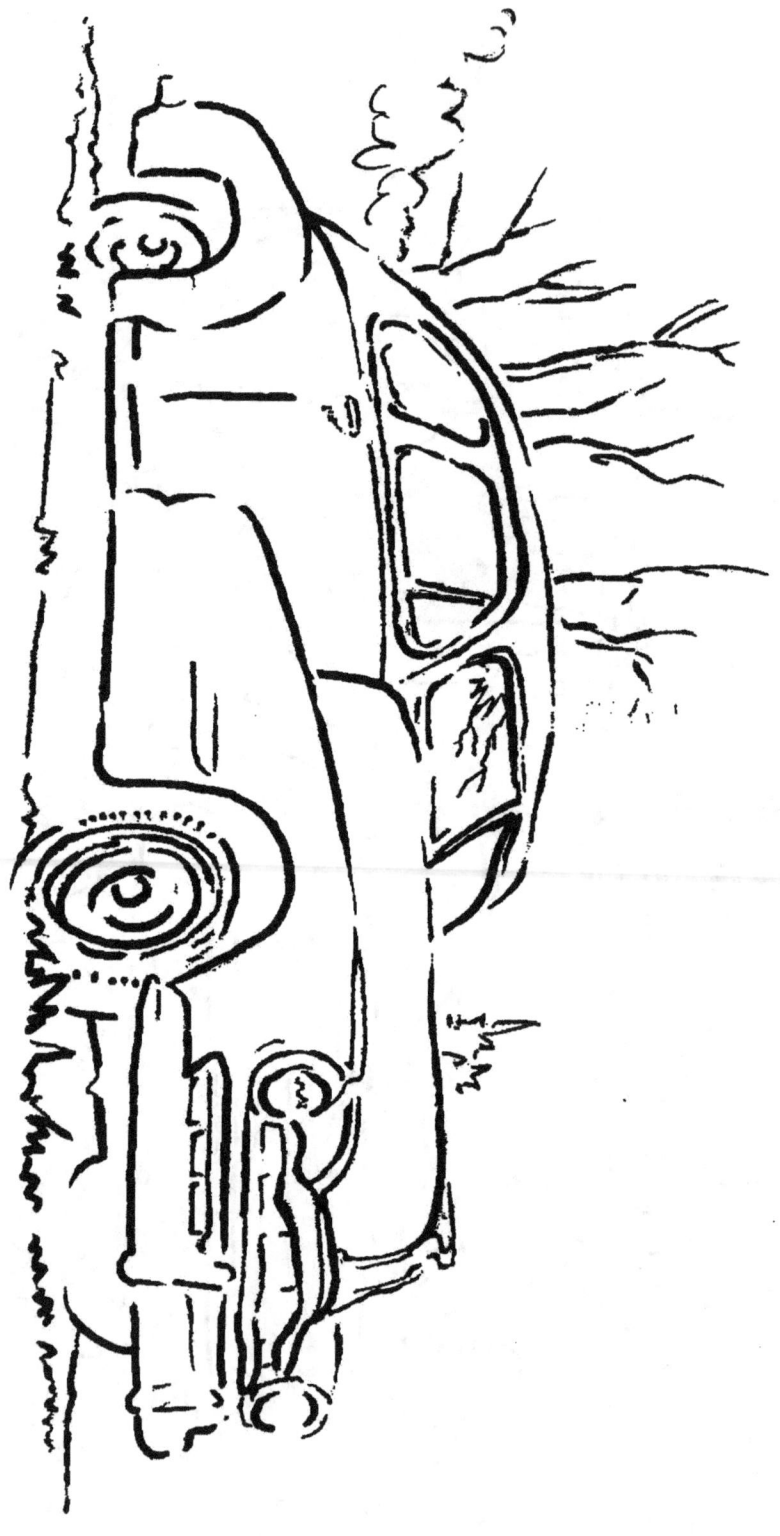

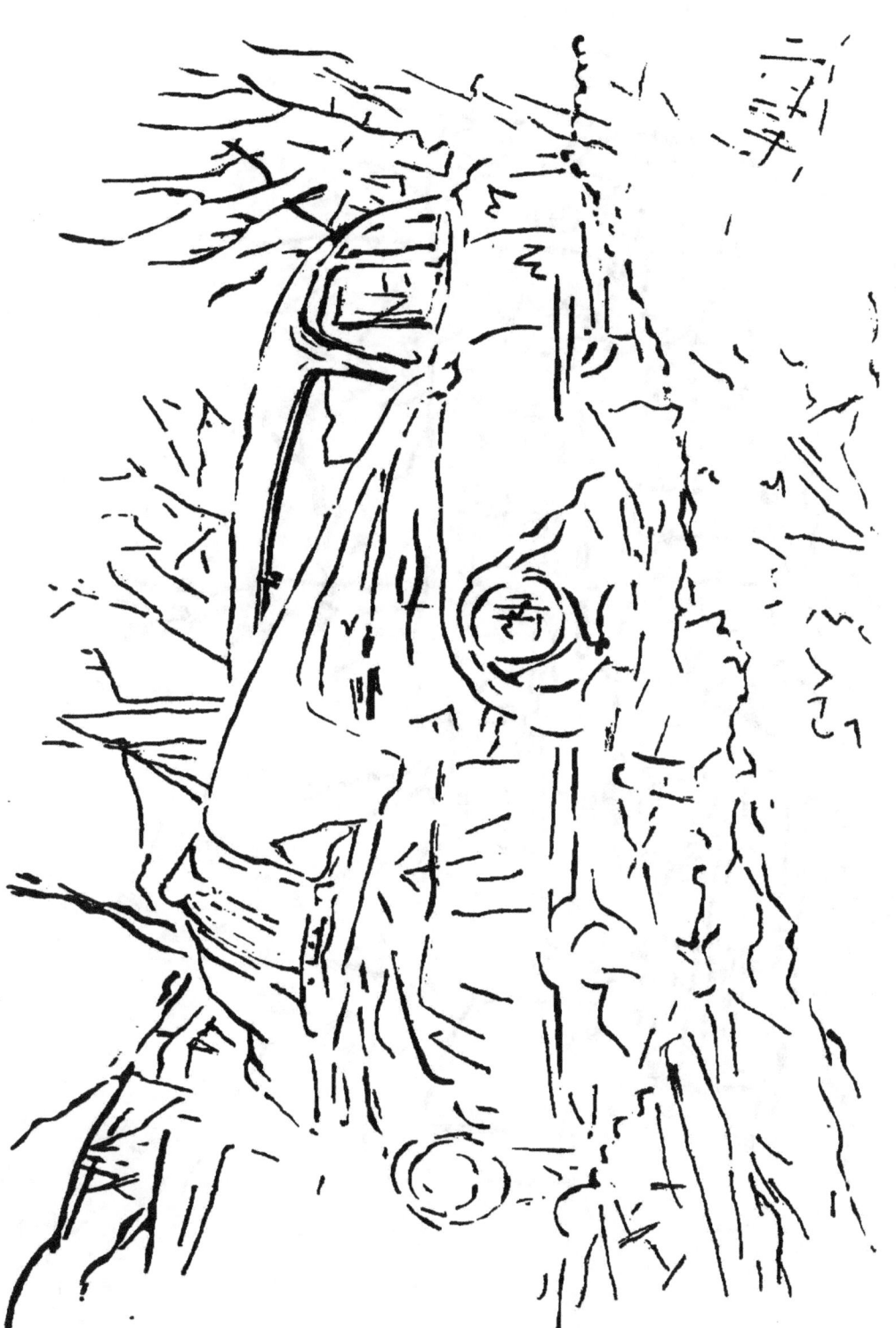

They were symbols of livelihood.

© MMI

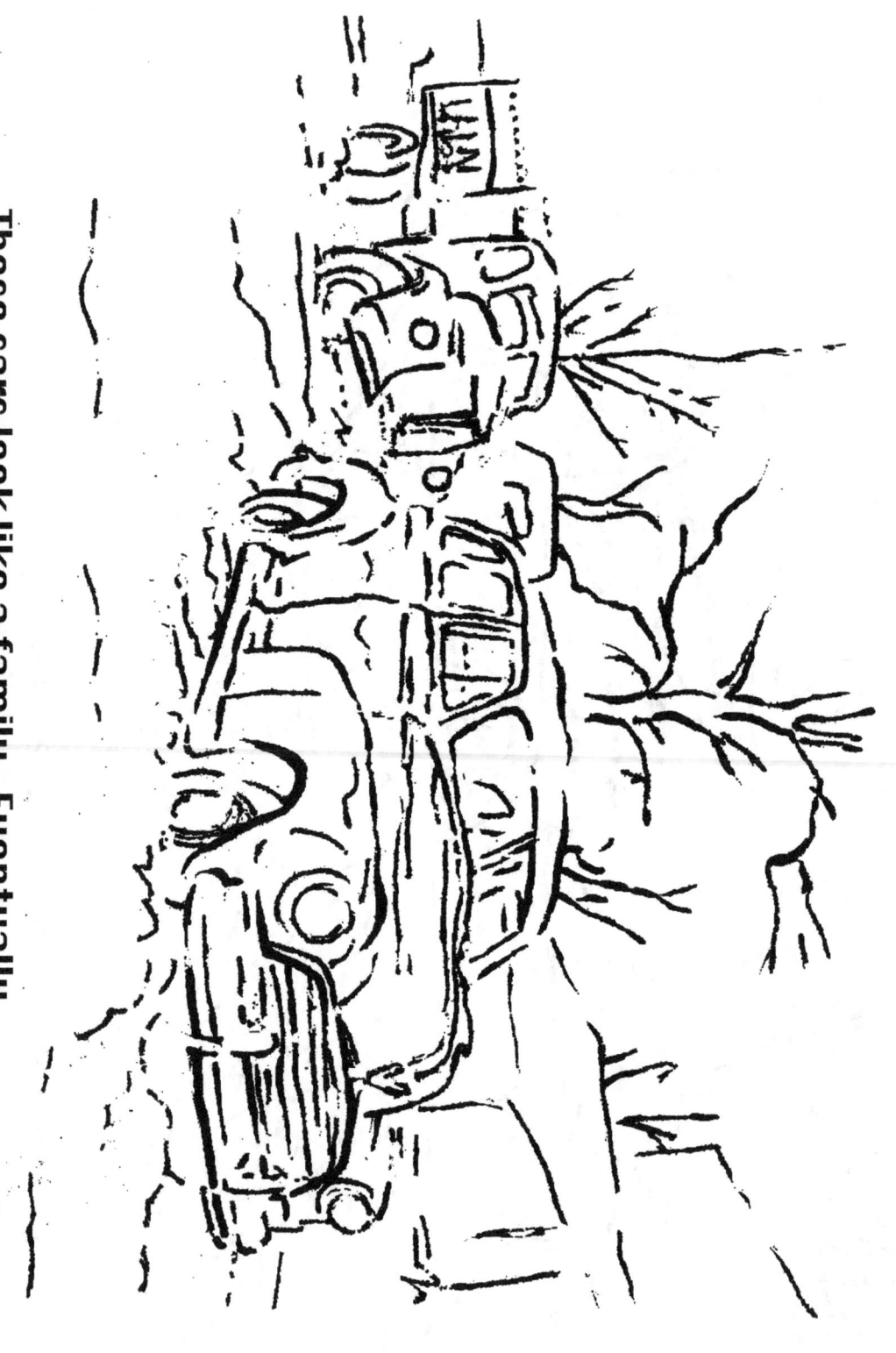

These cars look like a family. Eventually, families began to own two cars.

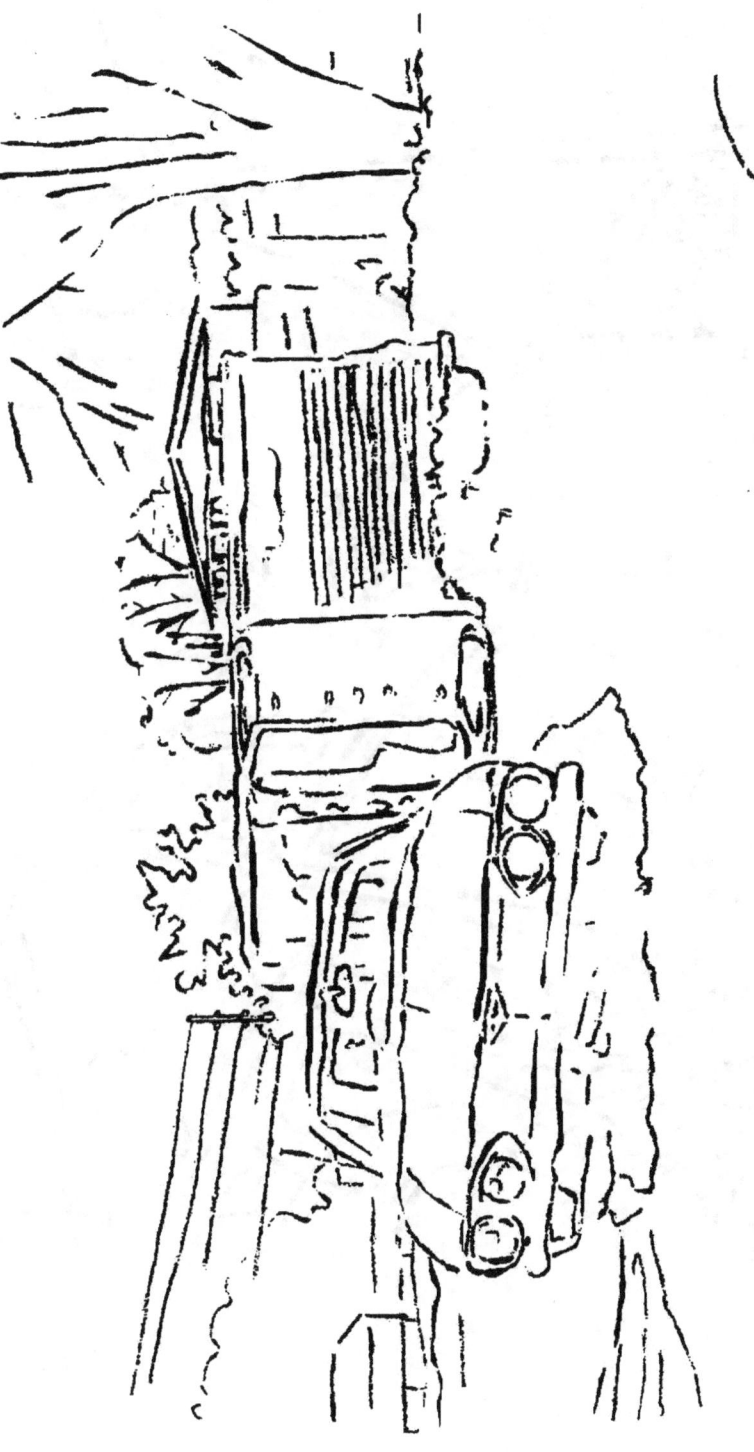

Then people had to build two–car garages!

Cars became symbols of
freedom and the open road.

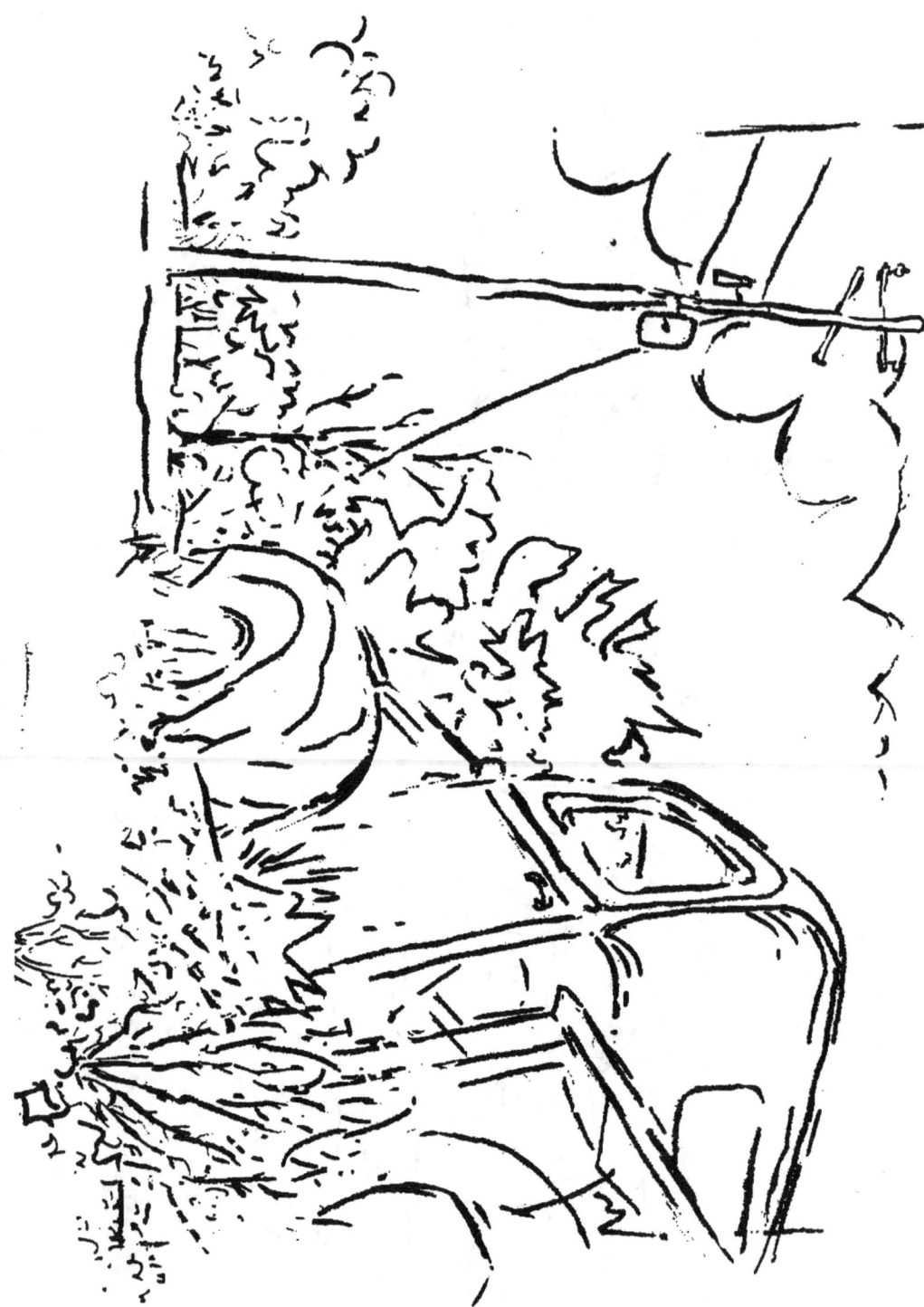

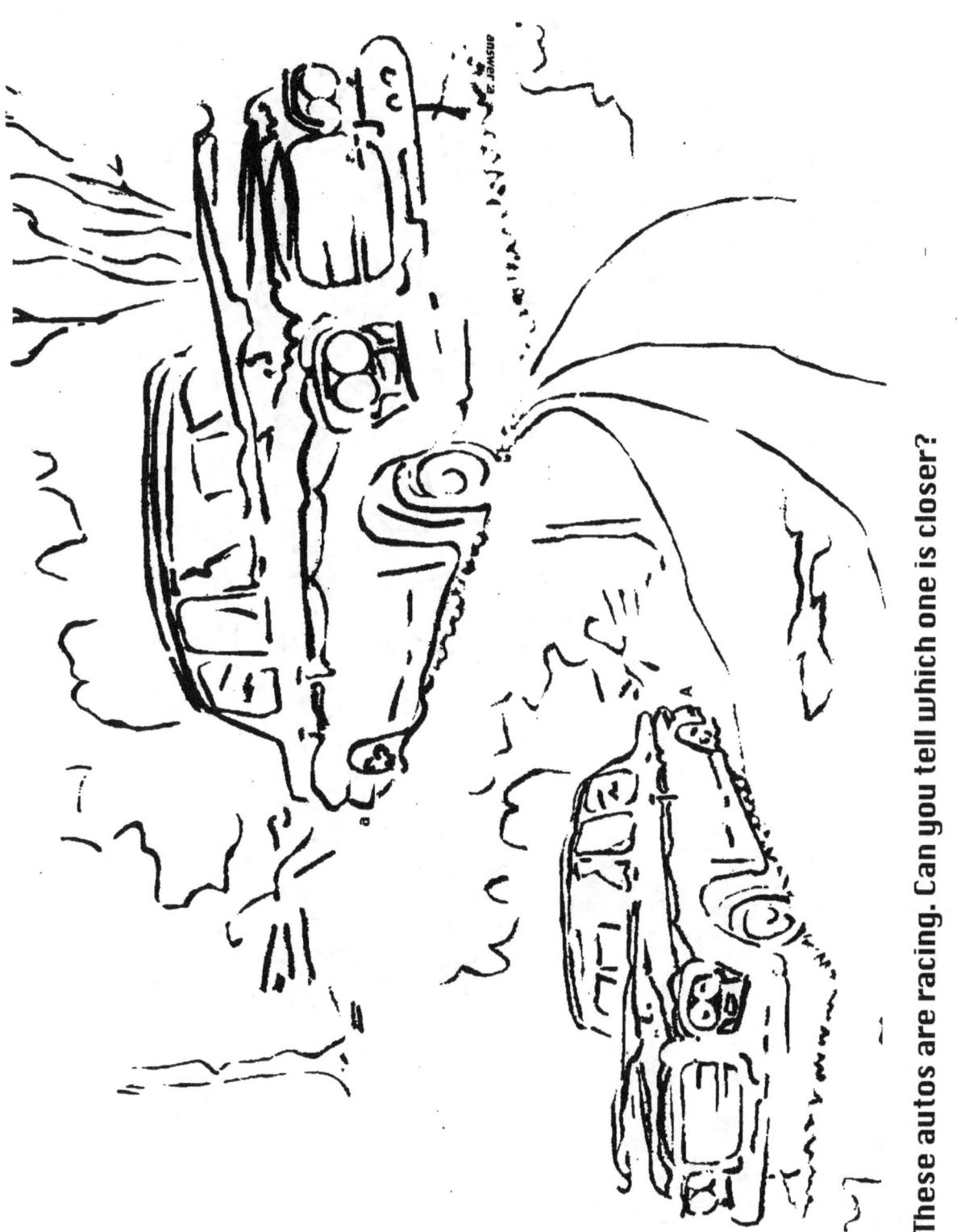

These autos are racing. Can you tell which one is closer?

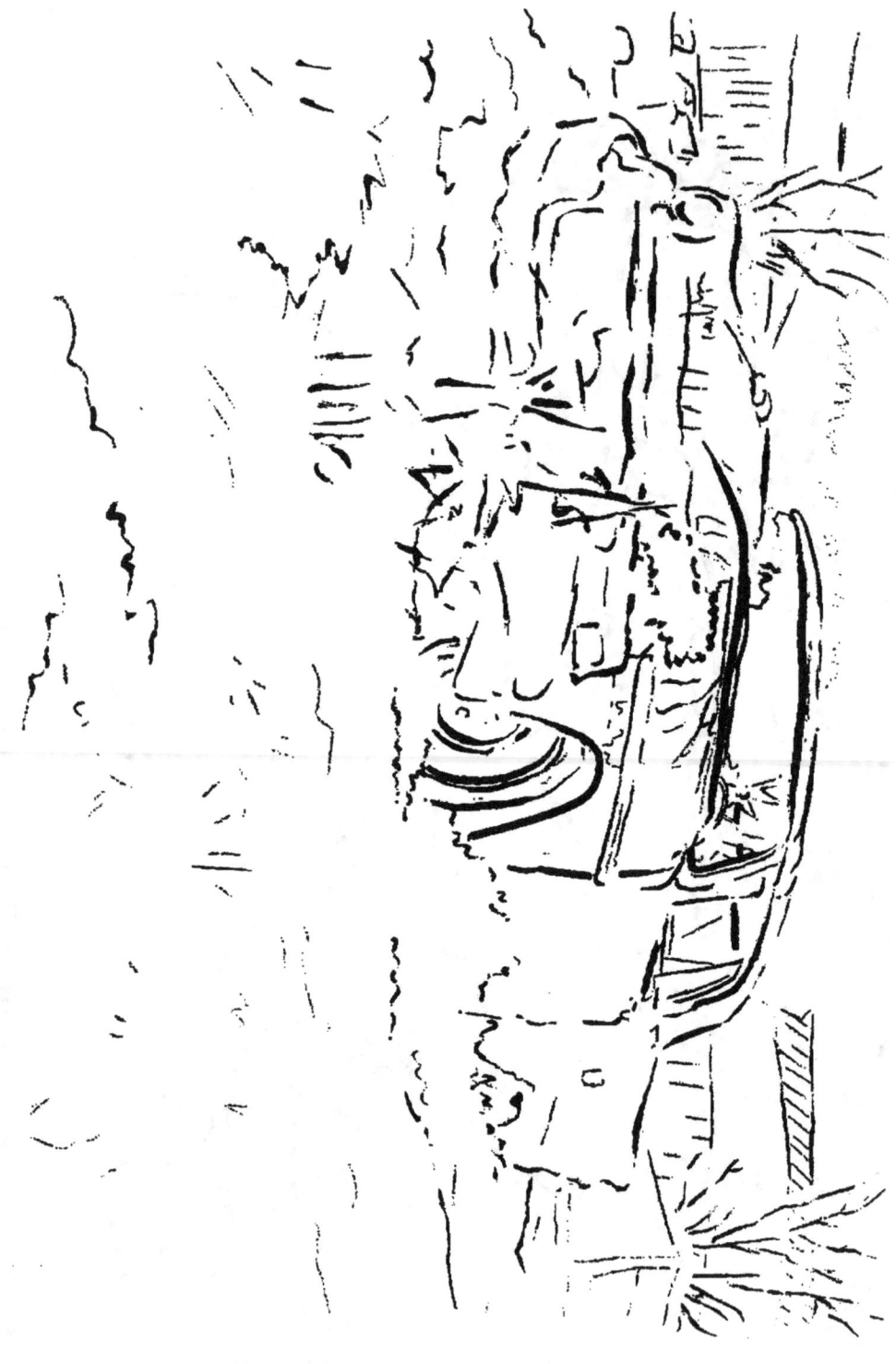

Then gas was rationed and became expensive because supplies were limited.

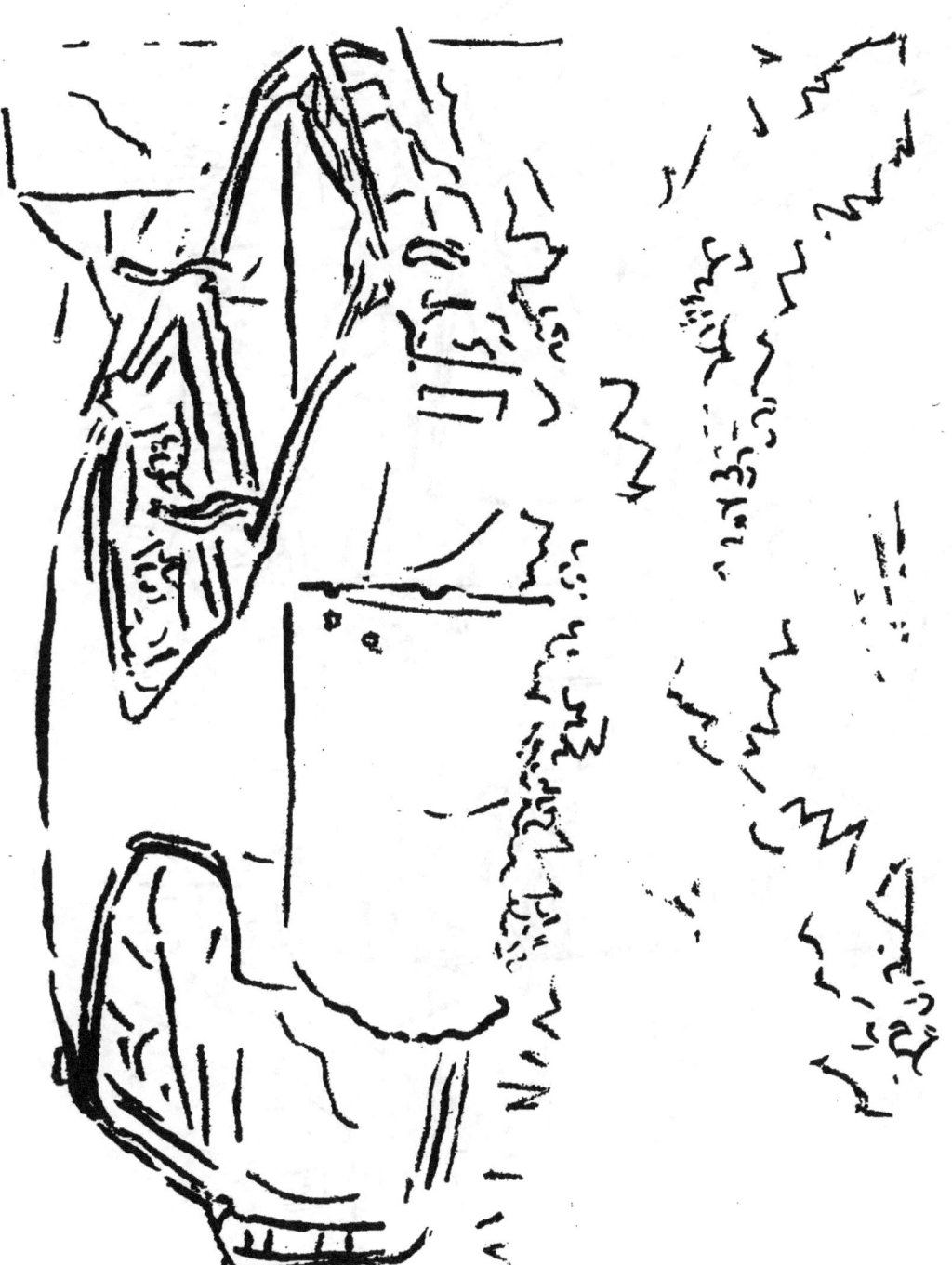

People abandoned their thirsty gas tanks.

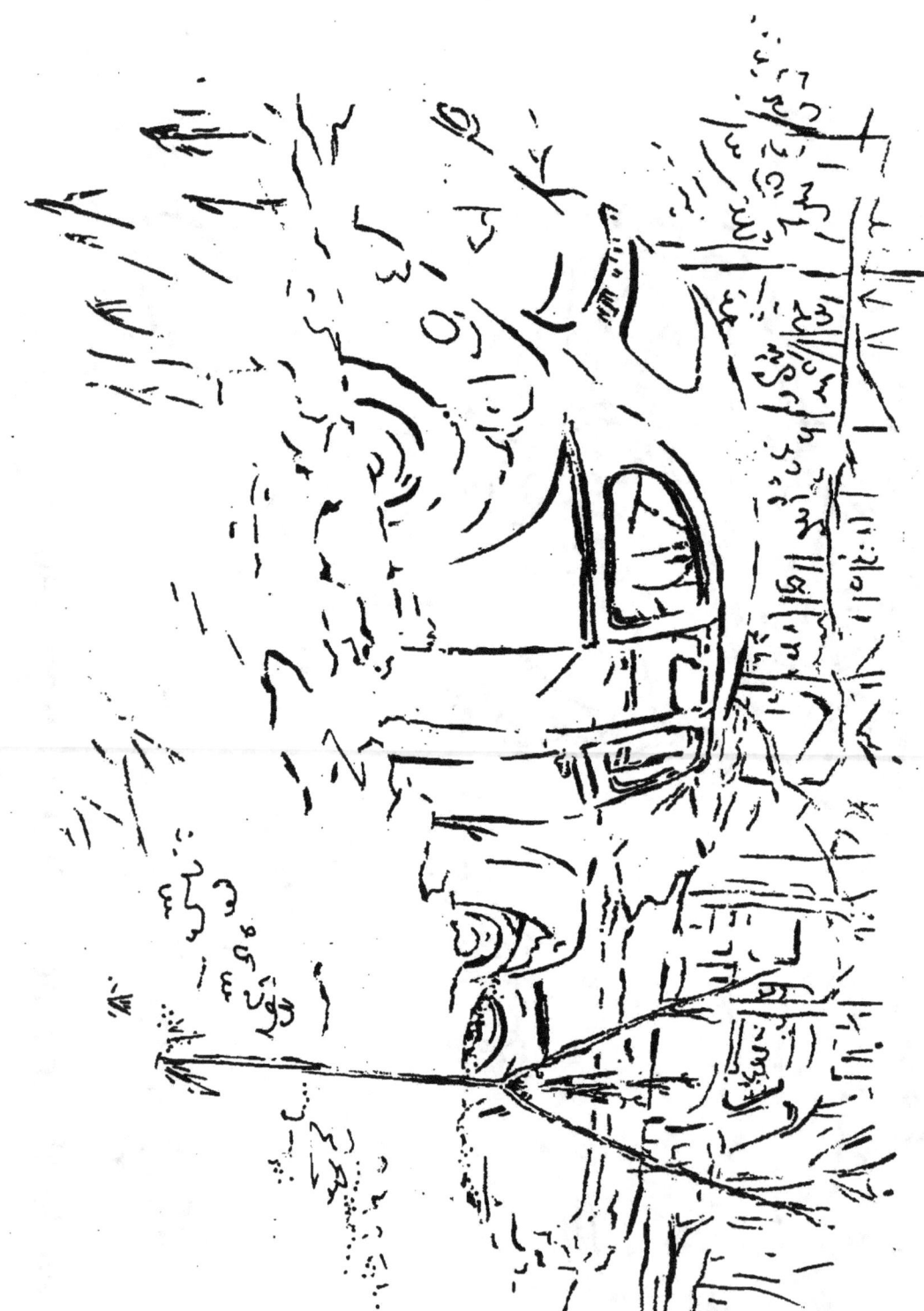

And bought compact vehicles instead.

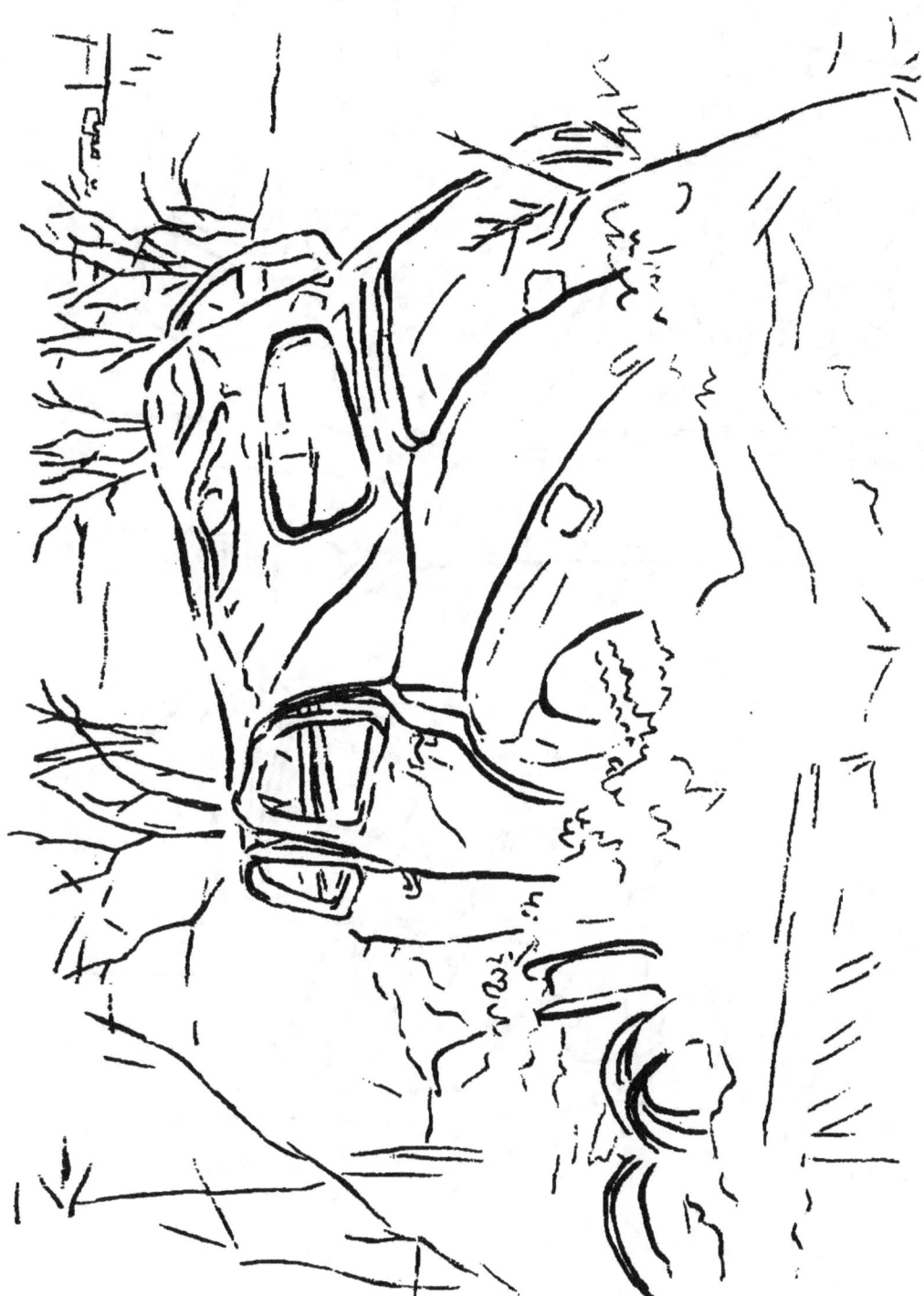

Smaller cars weren't always as safe.

This steel car was tough. It survived many snowstorms.

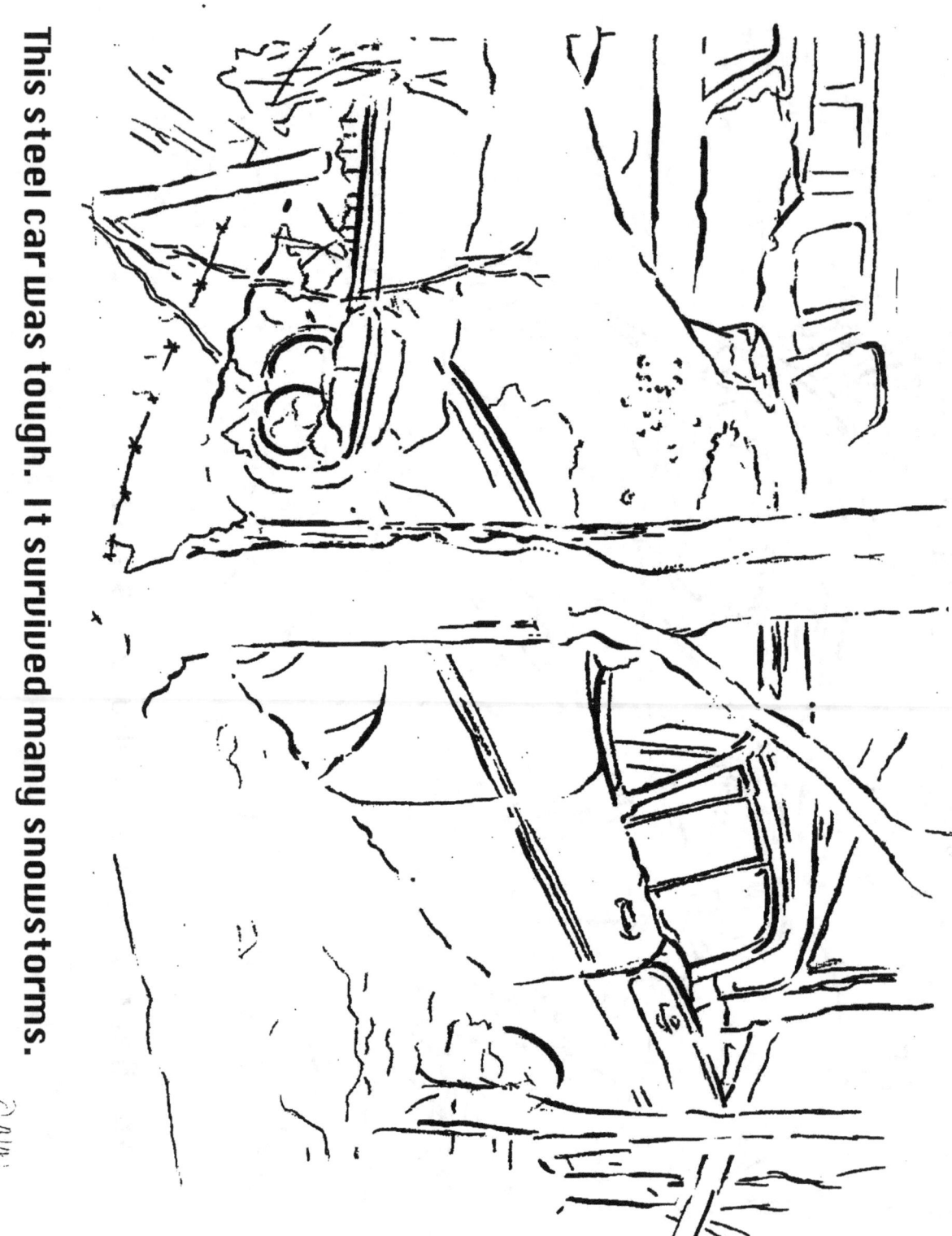

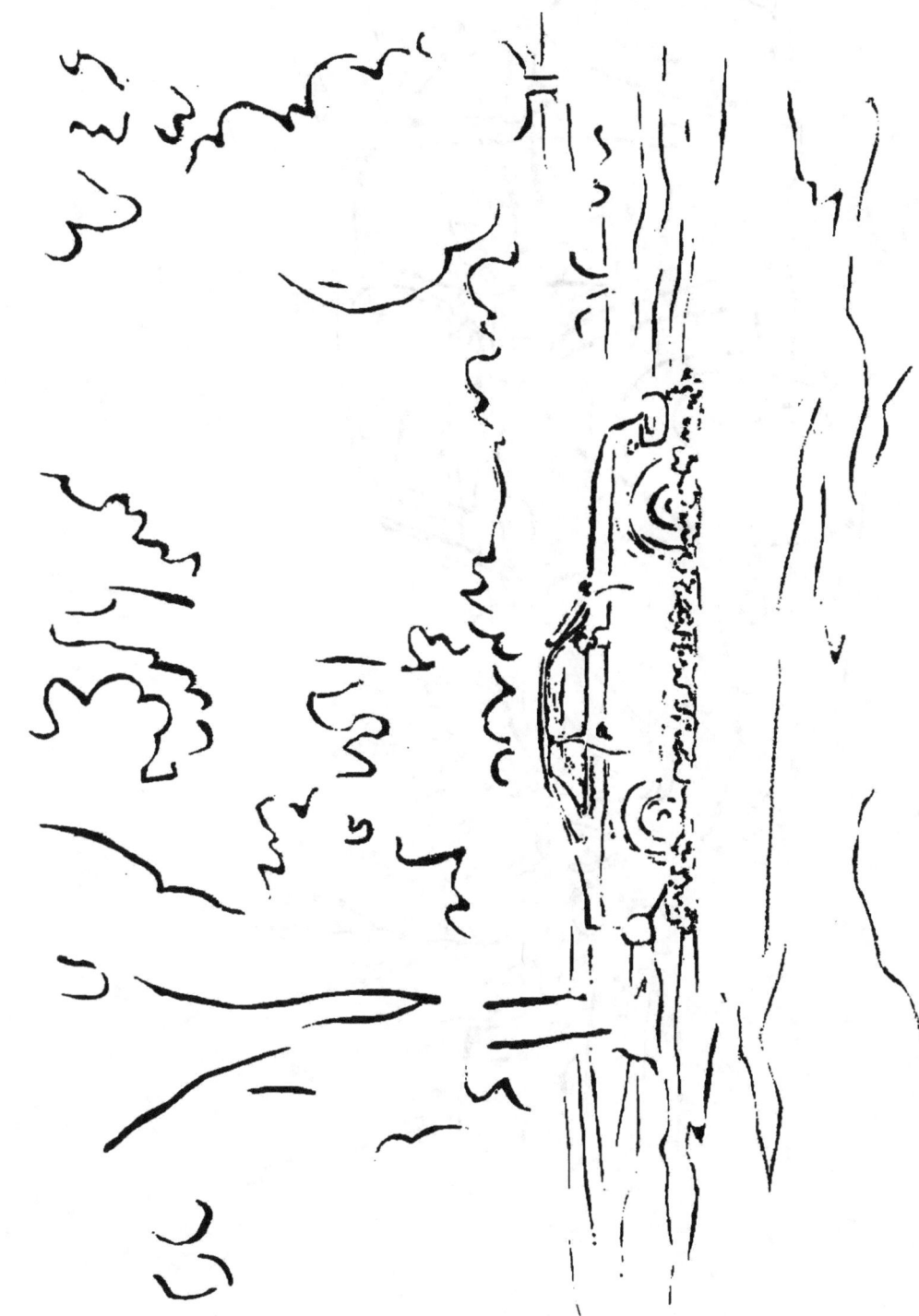

Today, consumers shop for style and speed.

© run

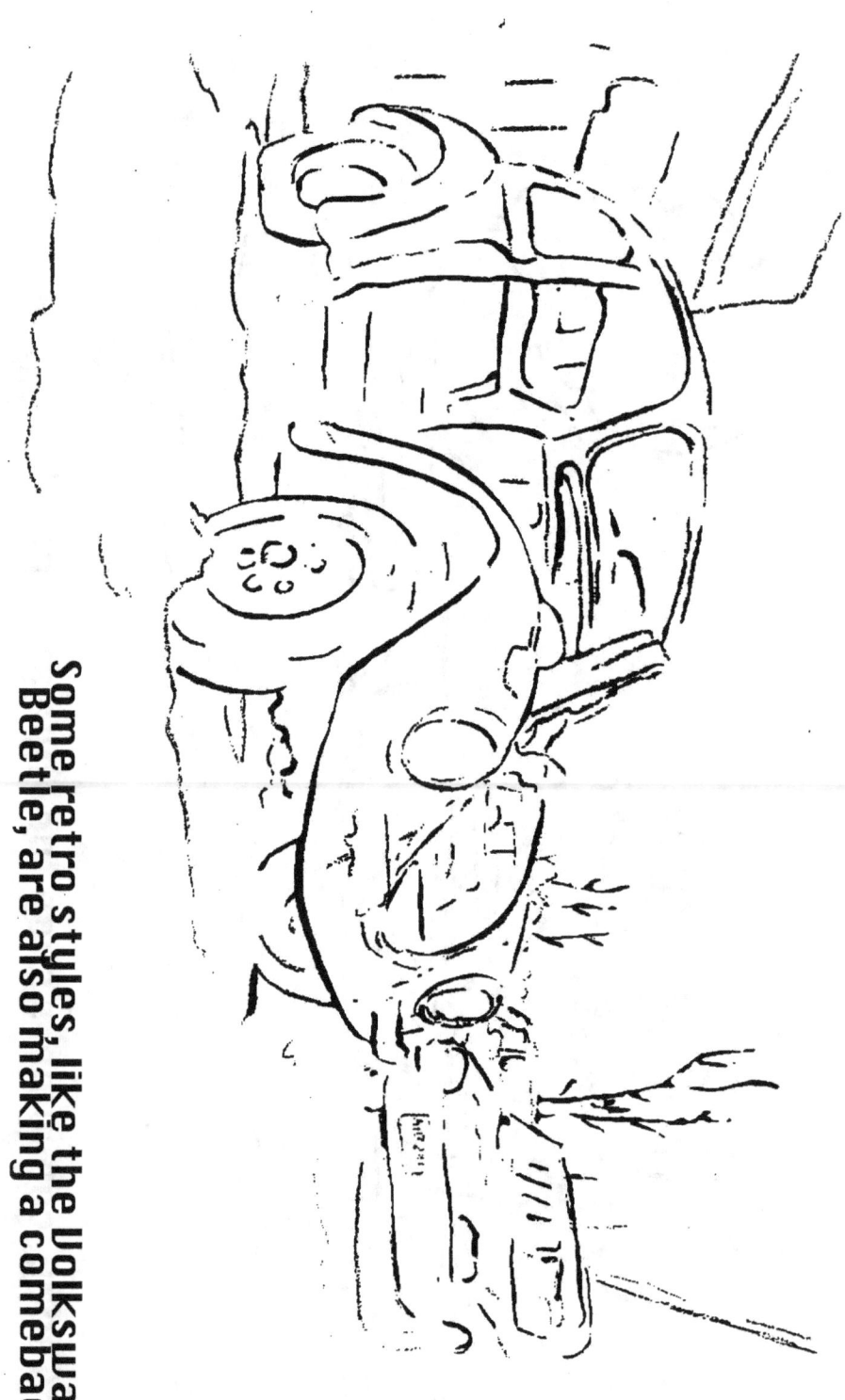

Some retro styles, like the Volkswagen Beetle, are also making a comeback.

22

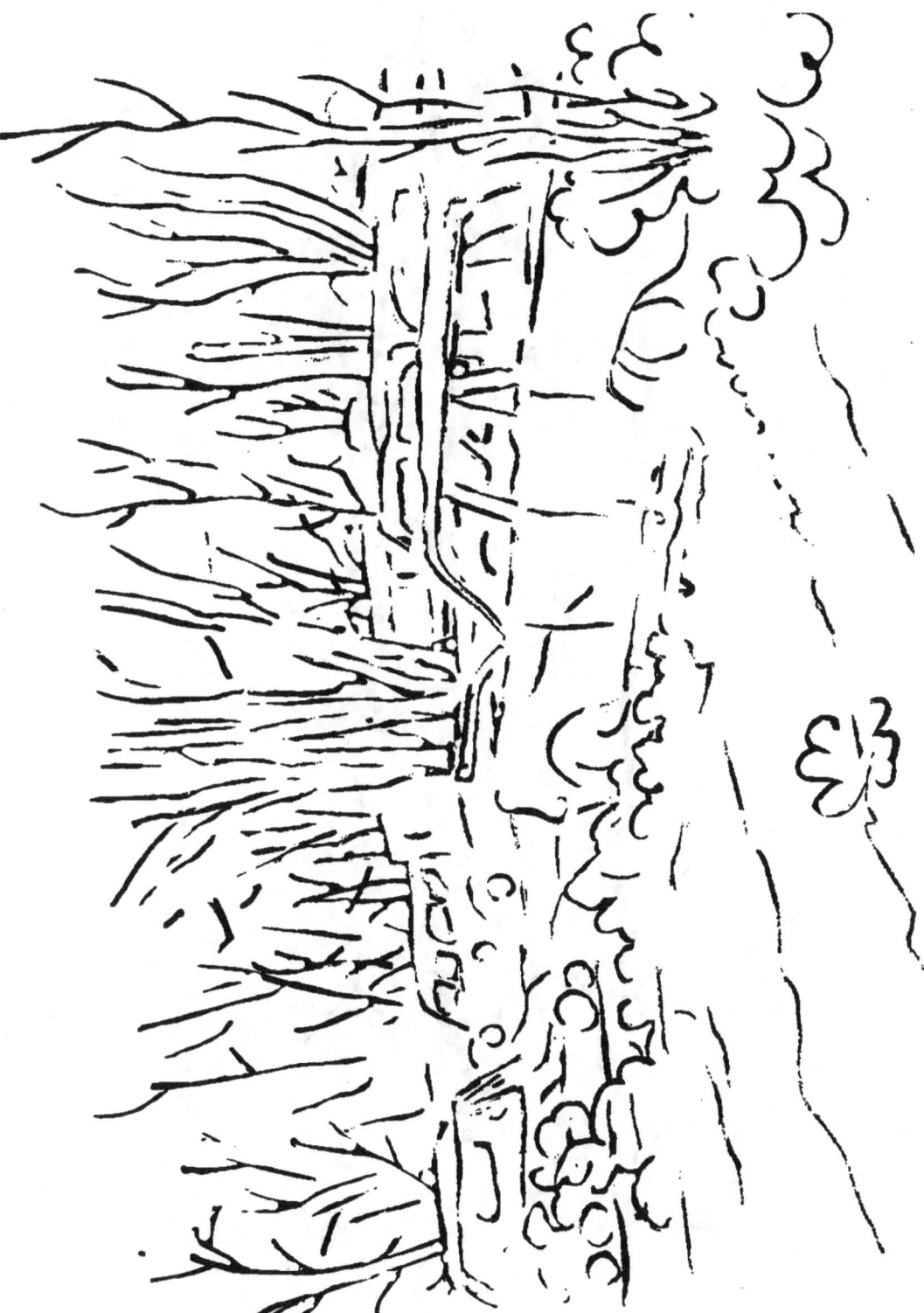

Nowadays, people dump their vehicles sooner, to buy flashier, newer ones.

In 2009, people were encouraged to give up their old cars and buy new ones. The old cars' engines were destroyed so they could not be reused.

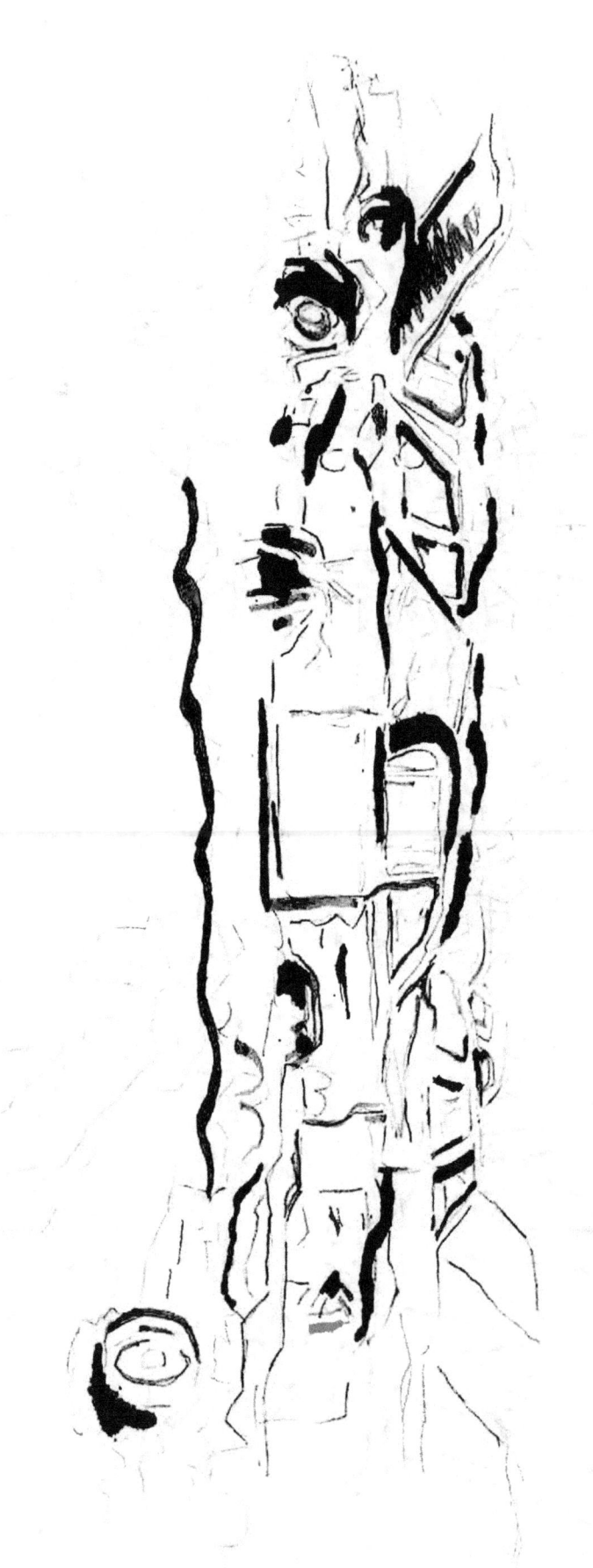

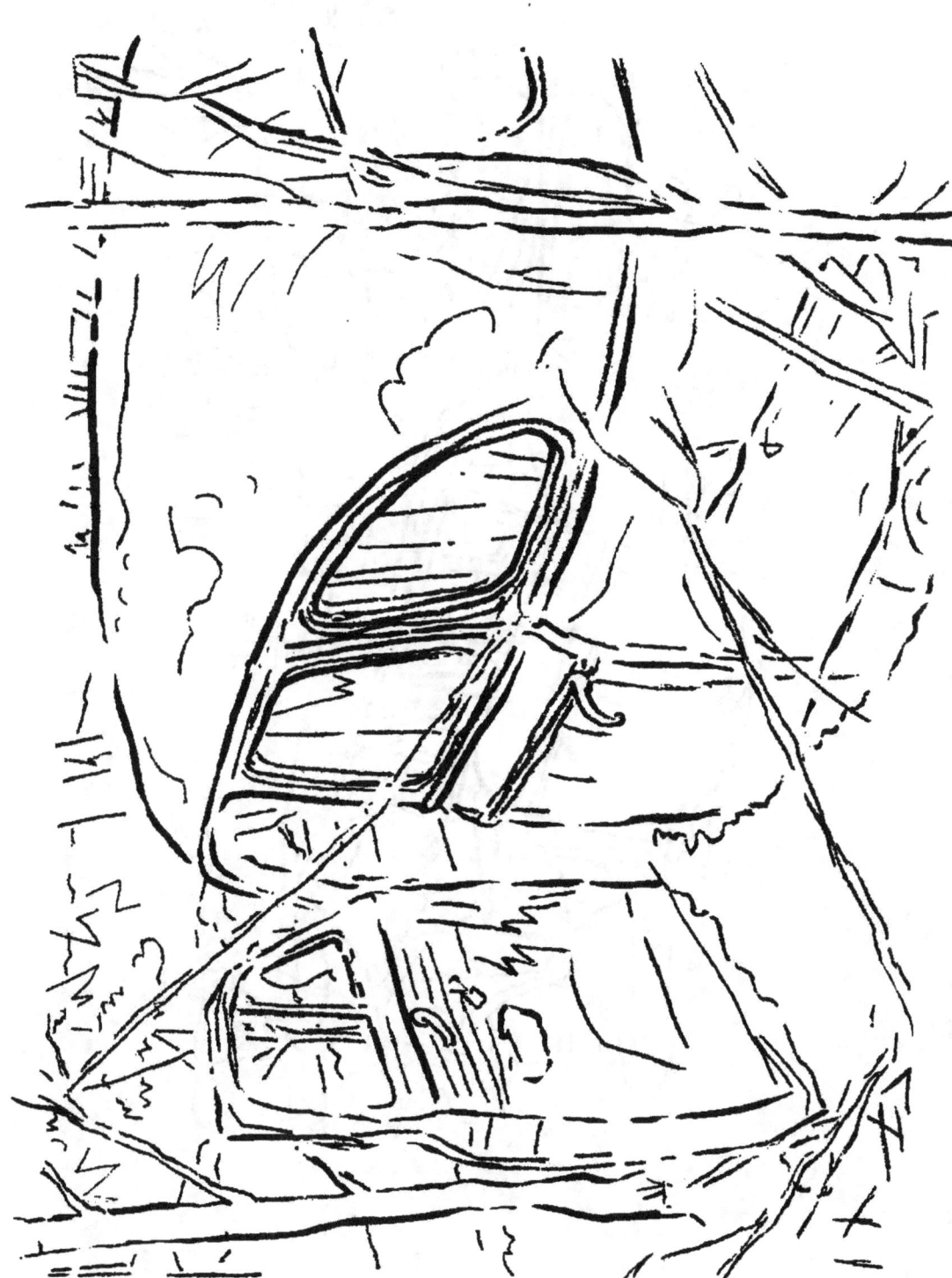

All cars have a story. Make up
a story about this car's life.

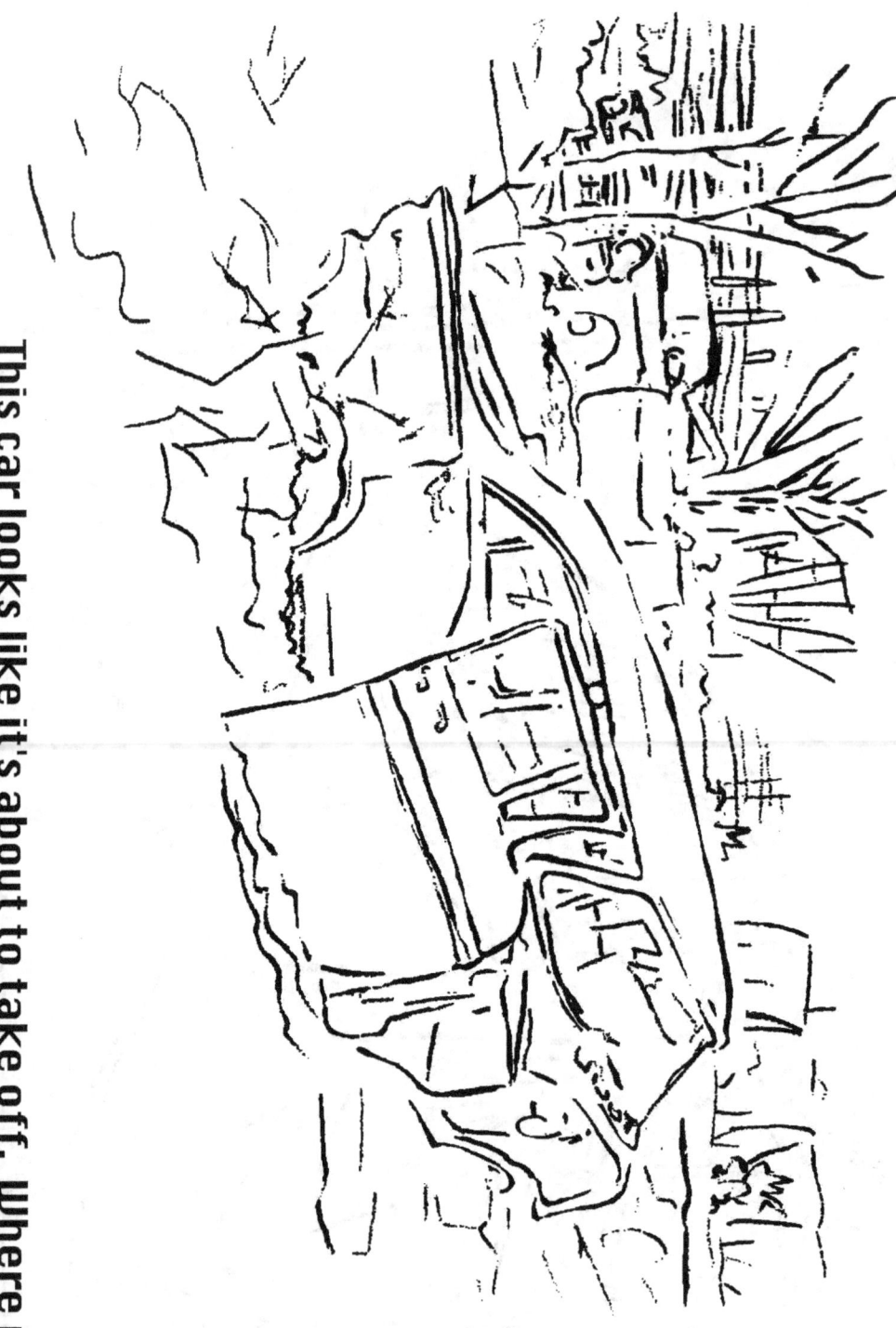

This car looks like it's about to take off. Where will our vehicles end up in the next millennium?

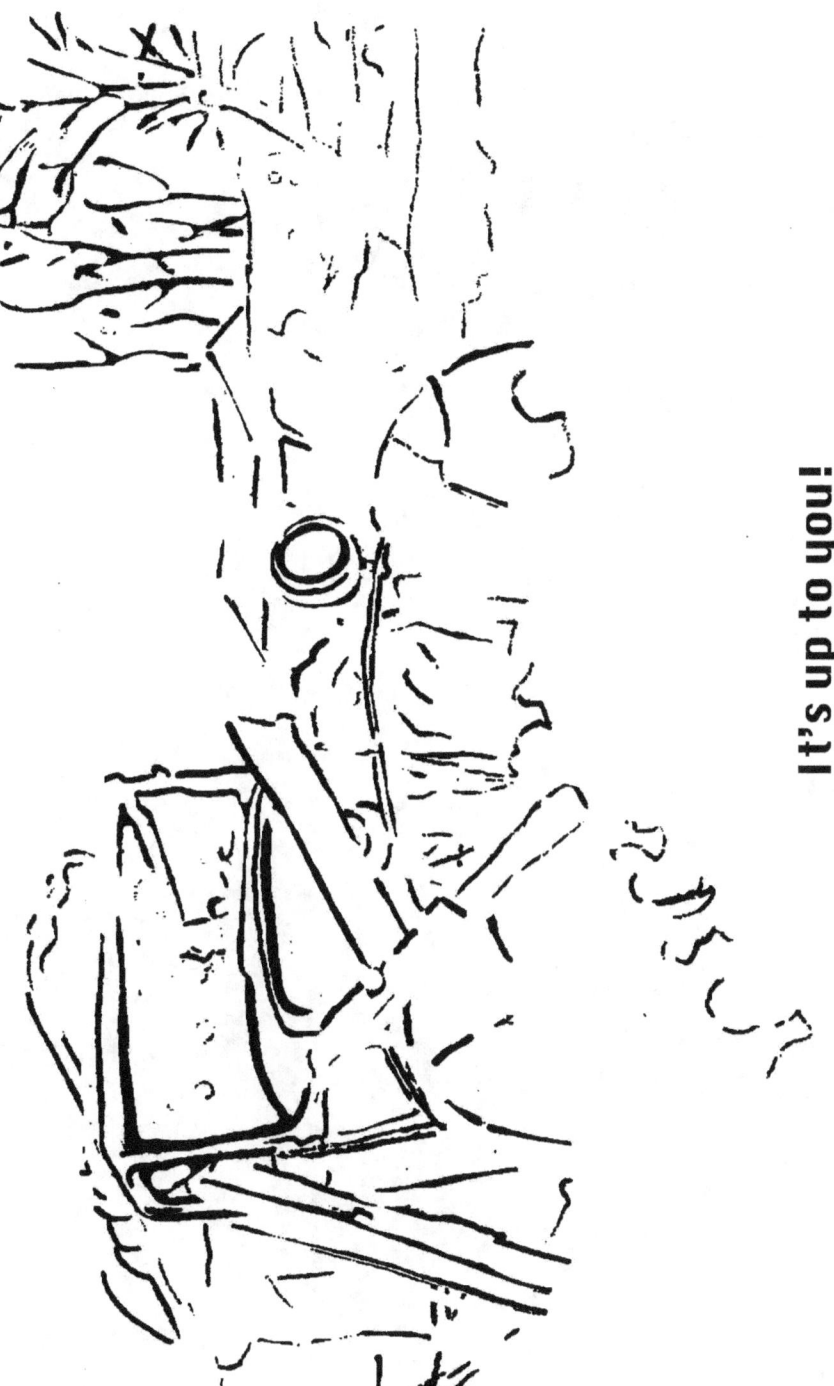

It's up to you!

www.ingramcontent.com/pod-product-compliance
Lightning Source LLC
Chambersburg PA
CBHW080859170526
45158CB00009B/2779